Lerner SPORTS

GREATEST OF ALL TIME PLAYERS

G.O.A.T. FOOTBALL KICKERS AND PUNTERS

Audrey Stewart

Lerner Publications ◆ Minneapolis

Lerner Publications Company
An imprint of Lerner Publishing Group, Inc.
241 First Avenue North
Minneapolis, MN 55401 USA

For reading levels and more information, look up this title at www.lernerbooks.com.

Main body text set in Aptifer Sans LT Pro.
Typeface provided by Linotype AG.

Library of Congress Cataloging-in-Publication Data

Names: Stewart, Audrey, author.
Title: G.O.A.T. football kickers and punters / Audrey Stewart.
Other titles: Greatest of all time football kickers and punters
Description: Minneapolis, MN : Lerner Publications, [2025] | Series: Lerner sports. Greatest of all time players | Includes bibliographical references and index. | Audience: Ages 7–11 | Audience: Grades 2–3 | Summary: "Kickers and punters are often overlooked members of football teams. But their jobs are extremely important. From booming punts to game-winning field goals, meet the NFL kickers and punters who rose above the rest"—Provided by publisher.
Identifiers: LCCN 2023049874 (print) | LCCN 2023049875 (ebook) | ISBN 9798765625835 (library binding) | ISBN 9798765628799 (paperback) | ISBN 9798765633847 (epub)
Subjects: LCSH: Football players—United States—Biography—Juvenile literature. | Football players—Rating of—United States—Juvenile literature.
Classification: LCC GV939.A1 S748 2025 (print) | LCC GV939.A1 (ebook) | DDC 796.332092/2—dc23/eng/20231122

LC record available at https://lccn.loc.gov/2023049874
LC ebook record available at https://lccn.loc.gov/2023049875

Manufactured in the United States of America
1 – CG – 7/15/24

TABLE OF CONTENTS

New England Patriots kicker Adam Vinatieri (*center*) made 29 game-winning kicks in his 24-season career.

BIG KICK!

The Carolina Panthers were playing the New England Patriots in the 2004 Super Bowl. Millions of people around the world watched the game. It was Carolina's first Super Bowl appearance. The Patriots were hoping for their second Super Bowl win in three years.

In the fourth quarter, the Panthers were losing 21–16. With less than seven minutes left, Panthers wide receiver Muhsin

FACTS AT A GLANCE

» **JUSTIN TUCKER** HOLDS THE NATIONAL FOOTBALL LEAGUE (NFL) RECORD FOR THE LONGEST FIELD GOAL AT 66 YARDS.

» **ADAM VINATIERI** IS THE NFL'S ALL-TIME LEADING SCORER WITH 2,673 POINTS.

» **JASON HANSON** SET 15 SCHOOL FOOTBALL RECORDS AT WASHINGTON STATE UNIVERSITY.

» **SHANE LECHLER** RANKS THIRD IN NFL HISTORY FOR YARDS PER PUNT WITH 47.6.

Muhammad caught an 85-yard touchdown pass. The play gave Carolina their first lead. The Patriots came back with a touchdown to go ahead 29–22. But the Panthers met this challenge with a game-tying touchdown.

With one minute left on the game clock, fans expected the game to go into overtime. But one minute was enough time

Adam Vinatieri

for New England and kicker Adam Vinatieri. He ran onto the field and kicked a game-winning 41-yard field goal with four seconds on the clock. The Patriots won 32–29 and went home with their second Super Bowl victory.

Kickers kick the ball to start each half and to start play after a score. Kickers also kick extra points and field goals. NFL kickers have good aim and can make kicks from long distances. Kickers are often the highest-scoring players on a football team.

Vinatieri celebrates his Super Bowl-winning field goal in the 2004 Super Bowl.

Punter Shane Lechler (*left*) led the NFL in total punting yards four times and yards per punt five times in his 18-year career.

Punters kick when their team chooses to give the ball to the other team. A team usually punts on fourth down when they are too far away to kick a field goal. This forces the other team to start their drive farther from the end zone. Most football teams have different players to kick and punt the ball. The best kickers and punters can make a huge impact on football games.

NO. 10 RAY GUY

In 1973, Ray Guy became the first punter in NFL history to be selected in the first round of the NFL Draft. Guy played his entire 14-year career with the Oakland Raiders and Los Angeles Raiders. He was best known for his very high kicks. Guy's high punts left the opposing team waiting longer to catch the ball, allowing the Raiders to advance down the field to defend. Guy's punts made scoring difficult for the Washington Redskins during the 1984 Super Bowl. The Raiders won 38–9.

In addition to punting, Guy handled the team's kickoffs and sometimes even played quarterback. He led the NFL in yards per punt three times, played in seven Pro Bowls, and won three Super Bowls with the Raiders. Guy retired from playing in 1986.

RAY GUY STATS

Games Played	207
Average Punt Yards	42.4
First-Team All-Pro Teams	3
Longest Punt	77 Yards

NO. 9 YALE LARY

The Detroit Lions picked the talented Yale Lary in the third round of the 1952 NFL Draft. Lary played with the Lions for 11 seasons as a punter and returner. Although he missed two seasons to serve in the US Army, Lary still ranks third in Lions history for total punting yards.

Lary could kick the ball long distances and great heights. While the other team was waiting for the ball, Lions players could run down the field to get into position for a quick tackle. The Lions had their best seasons with Lary as their punter. From 1952 to 1954, the Lions only lost seven games.

Lary was first in the NFL for yards per punt in 1959, 1961, and 1963. He helped the Lions win the NFL Championship in 1952, 1953, and 1957. He played in nine Pro Bowls, including every Pro Bowl from 1956 to 1962. Lary joined the Pro Football Hall of Fame in 1979.

YALE LARY STATS

Games Played	133
Average Punt Yards	44.3
First-Team All-Pro Teams	3
Longest Punt	73 Yards

NO. 8 JOHN CARNEY

Kicker John Carney started his NFL career in 1988 with the Tampa Bay Buccaneers. But his best years were with the San Diego Chargers from 1990 to 2000. He played 11 seasons with the Chargers and is their all-time leading scorer. Carney was also the NFL scoring leader in 1994 and was a First-Team All-Pro player.

In 1992, the Chargers went to the playoffs for the first time in 10 years. Their first-round playoff game against the Kansas City Chiefs was scoreless until the third quarter. After a Chargers touchdown, Carney kicked a 34-yard field goal to make the score 10–0. The Chargers won the game 17–0. Carney finished the season with 118 total points.

In 2009, Carney became the sixth player in NFL history to play in 300 career games. Carney won the 2010 Super Bowl with the New Orleans Saints. He played two more games with the Saints the next season before retiring from playing.

JOHN CARNEY STATS

Games Played	302
Field Goals Made	478
Points Scored	2,062
Longest Field Goal	54 Yards

NO. 7 JASON ELAM

Jason Elam joined the NFL in 1993 and played most of his career with the Denver Broncos. In his first season, Elam scored 119 points. He ranked seventh in the NFL for points scored. His total included a 54-yard field goal. It was the fourth-longest field goal in Broncos history.

In 1998, Elam played his best season. In a Broncos game against the Jacksonville Jaguars, Elam kicked a 63-yard field goal to give Denver a halftime lead. The kick tied the NFL record for the longest field goal at the time. The Broncos won the game 37–24. Elam finished the season with his second Pro Bowl appearance. He holds the record as the first player in NFL history to score more than 100 points in each of his first 11 seasons. He won back-to-back Super Bowls with the Broncos in 1998 and 1999.

JASON ELAM STATS

Games Played	263
Field Goals Made	436
Points Scored	1,983
Longest Field Goal	63 Yards

NO. 6 SHANE LECHLER

In 2000, his first season with the Oakland Raiders, Shane Lechler kicked 10 punts in a game against the San Diego Chargers. NFL teams usually punt about four times each game. Lechler finished the season with 65 punts for 2,984 yards. He helped the Raiders reach a 12–4 record and make it to the playoffs for the first time since 1993.

In 2003, Lechler and the Raiders played in the Super Bowl. Lechler had five punts in the game. The Raiders lost 48–21 to the Tampa Bay Buccaneers.

The next season was Lechler's best. He recorded a 73-yard punt, the longest in the NFL that season. He finished the year with 96 punts for 4,503 yards. Lechler led the NFL in punting yards in 2003, 2008, 2009, and 2017. He is ranked third all-time for average yards per punt with 47.6. He played in seven Pro Bowls and retired from playing in 2017.

SHANE LECHLER STATS

Games Played	286
Average Punt Yards	47.6
First-Team All-Pro Teams	6
Longest Punt	80 Yards

NO. 5 MATT PRATER

Matt Prater started his NFL career with the Denver Broncos. From 2008 to 2014, he was their starting kicker. Early in the 2008 season, Prater made a 56-yard field goal in a game against the Kansas City Chiefs. It was the third-longest field goal in Broncos history.

Prater's biggest moment came in the 2013 season. The Broncos were playing the Tennessee Titans. Prater set an NFL record when he kicked a 64-yard field goal to end the first half. The Broncos won 51–28. Prater's field goal broke the 63-yard field goal record first set by Tom Dempsey in 1970. Prater's record went unbroken until 2021.

Prater spent seven seasons with the Detroit Lions and has played for the Arizona Cardinals since 2021. He played in the 2013 and 2016 Pro Bowls. Prater has been the NFL Player of the Week 19 times.

MATT PRATER STATS

	Games Played	250
	Field Goals Made	401
	Points Scored	1,780
	Longest Field Goal	64 Yards

Stats are accurate through the 2023 NFL season.

NO. 4 STEPHEN GOSTKOWSKI

Stephen Gostkowski is the all-time leading scorer for the New England Patriots. The Patriots picked Gostkowski in the 2006 NFL Draft. He played 14 of his 15 NFL seasons with the team.

In 2017, Gostkowski set a Patriots record with a 58-yard field goal against the Carolina Panthers. Later that season, he set a new record with a career-high 62-yard field goal against the Oakland Raiders. It was the sixth-longest field goal in NFL history at that time.

In 2018, Gostkowski broke the record for most Super Bowl appearances by a kicker with six. Gostkowski led the NFL in scoring in 2008, 2012, 2013, 2014, and 2015. He won three Super Bowls and played in four Pro Bowls. He was a First-Team All-Pro player twice. Gostkowski kicked for the Tennessee Titans in 2020 and then retired from the NFL.

STEPHEN GOSTKOWSKI STATS

Games Played	219
Field Goals Made	392
Points Scored	1,875
Longest Field Goal	62 Yards

NO. 3 JASON HANSON

Jason Hanson set 15 school records at Washington State University. He still ranks second in school history with 328 career points, 63 field goals, and 139 extra points. In his senior season in 1991, Hanson kicked a 62-yard field goal. He joined the NFL the next year. After his first season with the Detroit Lions, Hanson was part of the NFL All-Rookie Team.

On November 12, 2000, in a game against the Atlanta Falcons, Hanson kicked a field goal in the fourth quarter to tie the game 10–10. With less than two minutes left on the game clock, he kicked another field goal. The kick gave the Lions a 13–10 victory.

Hanson played his entire 21-year career with the Detroit Lions. He holds the NFL record for most games played with one team and shares the record for most seasons with a single team. He is Detroit's all-time leading scorer with 2,150 points.

JASON HANSON STATS

Games Played	327
Field Goals Made	495
Points Scored	2,150
Longest Field Goal	56 Yards

NO. 2 ADAM VINATIERI

Adam Vinatieri played for the New England Patriots from 1996 to 2005. He joined the Indianapolis Colts in 2006 and played there until he retired from the NFL after the 2019 season.

Vinatieri was the NFL's scoring leader in 2004, and he holds several NFL records. He is the highest-scoring NFL player of all time with 2,673 points. Vinatieri kicked 44 field goals in a row without a miss to set another regular-season record. He also holds the record for most career field goals made with 599.

During his time in New England, Vinatieri had 18 game-winning field goals with less than a minute left on the game clock. He made almost 82 percent of his kicks with the Patriots and led the NFL in field goal percentage three times. Vinatieri won the Super Bowl with the Patriots in 2002, 2004, and 2005. He kicked game-winning field goals in the 2002 and 2004 Super Bowls. He won the big game again with the Colts in 2007.

ADAM VINATIERI STATS

Games Played	365
Field Goals Made	599
Points Scored	2,673
Longest Field Goal	57 Yards

NO. 1 JUSTIN TUCKER

No kicker in NFL history has been as successful as Justin Tucker. He makes nearly 90 percent of his kicks. In his first NFL season in 2012, Tucker made all 42 of his extra point tries. He only missed three out of 33 attempted field goals. He set a career-high in 2013 with 38 field goals made. He matched his own record in 2016.

At the start of the 2021 season, Tucker kicked the longest field goal in NFL history. The Ravens were playing the Detroit Lions. The Ravens were up 10–0 at halftime. Tucker kicked two field goals in the third quarter. But Detroit scored in the fourth quarter and took the lead 17–16. With three seconds on the game clock, Tucker kicked a 66-yard field goal to win the game and set a new NFL record.

JUSTIN TUCKER STATS

Stat	
Games Played	195
Field Goals Made	395
Points Scored	1,649
Longest Field Goal	66 Yards

Stats are accurate through the 2023 NFL season.

EVEN MORE G.O.A.T.

There have been so many amazing kickers and punters in NFL history. Choosing only 10 is a challenge. Here are 10 others who could have made the G.O.A.T. list.

No. 11	JIM BAKKEN
No. 12	MATT BRYANT
No. 13	TONI FRITSCH
No. 14	EDDIE MURRAY
No. 15	MARK MOSELEY
No. 16	PHIL DAWSON
No. 17	LOU GROZA
No. 18	GEORGE BLANDA
No. 19	JAN STENERUD
No. 20	MORTEN ANDERSEN

YOUR G.O.A.T.

It's your turn to make a G.O.A.T. list about kickers and punters. Start by doing research. Consider the rankings in this book. Then check out the Learn More section on page 31. Explore the books and websites to learn more about football players of the past and present.

You can search online for more information about great players too. Check with a librarian, who may have other resources for you. You might even try reaching out to football teams or players to see what they think.

Once you're ready, make your list of the greatest players of all time. Then ask people you know to make G.O.A.T. lists and compare them. Do you have players no one else listed? Are you missing anybody your friends think is important? Talk it over and try to convince them that your list is the G.O.A.T.!

GLOSSARY

draft: when teams take turns choosing new players

end zone: the area at each end of a football field where players score touchdowns

extra point: a score of one point made by kicking the ball over the crossbar; extra points can only be kicked after a touchdown

field goal: a score of three points made by kicking the ball over the crossbar

First-Team All-Pro: a team made up of each season's best NFL players

kickoff: a kick that puts the ball into play to start each half or after a score

Pro Bowl: the NFL's all-star game

punt: when a football player drops the ball and kicks it before it touches the ground

returner: a player who catches kickoffs and punts

rookie: a first-year player

LEARN MORE

Football Punter
https://www.rookieroad.com/football/positions/punter/

Hewson, Anthony K. *Football Records*. Lake Elmo, MN: Focus Readers, 2020.

Levit, Joe. *G.O.A.T. Football Teams*. Minneapolis: Lerner Publications, 2021.

Lowe, Alexander. *G.O.A.T. Football Quarterbacks*. Minneapolis: Lerner Publications, 2023.

Top 10 Kickers
https://www.profootballhof.com/football-history/top-10-kickers/

What Is a Kicker in Football?
https://footballadvantage.com/football-kicker/

INDEX

PHOTO ACKNOWLEDGMENTS

Image credits: Boston Globe/Contributor/Getty Images, p.4; Boston Globe/ Contributor/Getty Images, p.5; Boston Globe/Contributor/Getty Images, p.6; Doug Pensinger/Staff/Getty Images, p.7; Focus On Sport/Contributor/Getty Images, p.8; Focus On Sport/Contributor/Getty Images, p.9; Bettmann/Contributor/Getty Images, p.10; The Enthusiast Network/Contributor/Getty Images, p.11; Focus On Sport/Contributor/Getty Images, p.12; Focus On Sport/Contributor/Getty Images, p.13; The Sporting News/Contributor/Getty Images, p.14; Sporting News Archive/ Contributor/Getty Images, p.15; Ezra Shaw/Staff/Getty Images, p.16; Diamond Images/Contributor/Getty Images, p.17; Donald Miralle/Stringer/Getty Images, p.18; Cooper Neill/Contributor/Getty Images, p.19; Tom Szczerbowski/Contributor/ Getty Images, p.20; Mike Ehrmann/Staff/Getty Images, p.21; George Gojkovich/ Contributor/Getty Images, p.22; Leon Halip/Contributor/Getty Images, p.23; Icon Sports Wire/Contributor/Getty Images, p.24; Stacy Revere/Contributor/Getty Images, p.25; Rob Carr/Staff/Getty Images, p.26; Andy Lyons/Staff/Getty Images, p.27

Cover: Jason Miller/Contributor/Getty Images; Scott Cunningham/Stringer/Getty Images, Patrick Smith/Staff/Getty Images